Original title:
The Locket's Light

Copyright © 2025 Creative Arts Management OÜ
All rights reserved.

Author: Mariana Leclair
ISBN HARDBACK: 978-1-80586-171-3
ISBN PAPERBACK: 978-1-80586-643-5

Enshrined Moments

In a box of trinkets, I found a pair,
A shiny little doodad with a curious stare.
I clipped it on my cat, oh what a sight,
He strutted 'round the house like a true knight.

A photo of Auntie with cake on her face,
Her smile so wide, it takes up all the space.
I keep it near, for a giggle or two,
When the mood feels heavy, it brightens the view.

A dance with my shoes tied, oh what a fall,
The tumble brought laughter, we all had a ball.
The world feels much lighter when laughter takes flight,
In pockets of joy, the day feels just right.

So treasure those moments, let whimsies abound,
For life is a circus, with joy all around.
With giggles and chuckles, let's turn up the cheer,
Enshrined in our hearts, they'll always be near.

Luminescence in the Dark

In shadows deep, a glow will play,
It dances 'round, a cheeky sway.
A lamp that's off, yet shines so bright,
With jellybeans, it wins the night.

Your shoes are paired, but one's gone rogue,
It's hiding where the cats would stroll.
Upon a shelf, in fruitcake's fate,
Who knew that food could fascinate?

Golden Threads of Nostalgia

A sweater worn, three sizes small,
Its arms can barely hold my brawl.
Yet memories cling, like tape on skin,
To laugh at battles I can't win.

Old photos tease with silly smirks,
Of hairstyles bold and fashion quirks.
I once was chic, or so I thought,
Now cringing hard at what I bought.

A Flicker of Familiarity

A toast to friends with drinks in hand,
We spill our tales, oh isn't it grand?
The pizza burns, the cheese is goo,
But laughter's hot and always true.

A cat that leaps on table tops,
Adjourned discussions of which that stops.
Yet in this chaos, hearts collide,
Sylvester's here, with crazy pride.

Chasing Faint Glimmers

A spark of joy, a fleeting quest,
For cookies stolen, one can guess.
We roam the night, like dogs in flight,
Through starlit trails and soft moonlight.

My friend just tripped, a grand ballet,
He said a word, I can't repeat today.
With laughter loud, our voices blend,
Chasing dreams where giggles mend.

Beneath the Silent Glow

Underneath that quiet spark,
A cat wearing shades, oh what a lark!
It wobbles and dances, full of glee,
Chasing its tail, as wild as can be.

A mouse takes notes, in a tiny chair,
Thinking of cheese, without a care.
The stars giggle in their silver hues,
While the sofa snores in its old blue shoes.

Reflections in Twilight

In a puddle, a frog does pose,
Decked in a crown made of garden hose.
It croaks a tune, quite out of place,
Wishing for flies but catching some grace.

A snail on skis, just gliding by,
Winking at the clouds drifting high.
Naps in between, that's its big plan,
While a sleepy gnome counts to ten, then ran.

The Keeper's Embrace

An owl with glasses reads a tome,
Preferring midnight over its home.
With a hoot and a wink, it flies around,
Stealing snacks that are nowhere to be found.

Bears sharing jokes near the old oak tree,
Comically arguing who's funnier, me!
The keeper chuckles, waving a pie,
As squirrels bicker, asking, 'Who ate the fry?'

In the Shadow of Radiance

A raccoon suited up in a tux,
Stealing shiny things, oh what luck!
While the shadows giggle at his spree,
Wondering if he'd ever just flee.

A parrot squawks, wearing a bow,
Telling all tales of a friend named Joe.
With laughter echoing under the moon,
The night sings songs of a cartoon tune.

Whispers of Radiance

In a pocket, treasures hum,
Winking trinkets, oh what fun!
Giggles caught in silver charm,
Secrets wrapped, a quirky arm.

Twinkling tales that twist and spin,
Silly dances, grins begin.
This little gem holds whispers bright,
Wilder than a kite in flight.

Memories Encased in Silver

A silver band from ages past,
Captured laughs that never last.
Blink and you'll miss a silly jest,
Memories packed, it's truly blessed.

Each glint a tale, each twinkle a tease,
Ticklish moments carried with ease.
Wrapped in laughter, a gleeful plight,
Shining stories kept in light.

Glimmers of Hidden Affection

Behind the clasp, a giggle hides,
Little treasures that never bide.
Winks exchanged like silly notes,
Each glimmer floats, oh how it gloats!

Curled up whispers, soft and sweet,
Tickling feet in merry beat.
Jokes in silver, laughter bright,
Glimmers dance in joyful flight.

Echoes from a Timepiece Heart

In ticking beats, a jest unfolds,
Time whispers of the dreams it holds.
Witty chimes and playful glee,
Echoes bounce, they're wild and free.

Moments tick-tock like a clown,
Smiles abound, never a frown.
The heart's a joker, bright as day,
With every tick, it finds a way.

A Veil of Memories

Once I lost my favorite charm,
Thought my heart would face alarm.
But it turned out, with a laugh,
It was in my other half's photograph.

Every picture tells a tale,
Watching memories sail,
Through giggles and playful jest,
Who knew being absent was the best?

Phosphorescent Bonds

In a box, secrets glow bright,
Like fireflies in the night.
I tried to eat one, oh what a scene,
Turns out they taste like something green!

We gathered laughter as we spun,
With glowing trinkets, we had such fun.
But the best times were not bought,
Just memories and light we sought.

Wishes Suspended in Time

Jars of wishes lined the shelf,
I mistook one for myself.
Tried to make my dreams appear,
Ended up with a rubber duck here!

Each wish a giggle, each laugh a twist,
Who knew wishes could play tryst?
Time stood still, but we flew high,
Trading dreams and a pie in the sky.

Dancers in the Moonlight

Two shadows twirl under the glow,
With missteps that steal the show.
Each laugh crackles through the air,
As we dance without a care.

Moonbeams join in our delight,
Making fools of us all night.
Clumsy feet and hearts so free,
Forever dancing, it's you and me.

Ethereal Connections

In a pocket, secrets hide,
A shiny trinket, in a ride.
It sparkles bright in the sun,
Who knew it could be such fun?

A laugh, a wink, a silly face,
This charm, it's a holy place.
Love messages, just a glance,
Oh, the joy of a romance!

Crafted in Light

It flickers like a firefly,
In every laugh, a lullaby.
Hopping from here to there,
Bringing smiles everywhere.

Like popcorn popping in the night,
Every moment feels just right.
Crafted with giggles, pure delight,
Unseen magic, shining bright!

The Glow Within the Silence

A shiny thing with a twist,
Its humor?
It can't be missed!
Winks and nods, a playful tease,
Laughter dances with the breeze.

In quiet rooms, it softly glows,
Telling tales that nobody knows.
With each chuckle, it starts to beam,
We're all part of this funny dream!

A Dance of Illuminations

Under the stars, we make a scene,
A quirky glow, oh what a sheen!
Dancing shadows twist and twirl,
Underneath its sparkling swirl.

Check your pockets, oh so merry,
This little trinket's quite the cherry.
It tickles hearts where laughter flows,
Join the fun, the light still grows!

Celestial Keepsake

In a box, so small and round,
A treasure hidden to be found.
With laughter and a silly grin,
Who knew that joy could fit within?

Dancing stars in a zany twirl,
Whispers of giggles, watch them whirl.
Each clasp unlocks a memory's tease,
With mischief wrapped in a cosmic breeze.

Tints of Treasured Time

A snapshot caught in a playful stare,
Colors splashed without a care.
Each hue a laugh, a wink, a jest,
In moments where we feel our best.

A canvas framed with joys untold,
Stories shared, and memories bold.
We paint our days with light-hearted cheer,
Tints of time that always endear.

Echoes of Affection

A shout, a laugh, a friendly poke,
In the midst of playful joke.
Echoes bounce around the room,
Filling hearts like springtime bloom.

Each giggle curls like a wispy curl,
Bouncing back in this crazy whirl.
With every chuckle, joy is found,
In the echoes that so sweetly sound.

The Secrets We Hold

Hidden giggles in whispers soft,
Stories of mayhem loft and scoff.
Each secret shared, a light-hearted laugh,
Life's quirky moments, oh what a path!

In solemn hush, a wink exchanged,
Mischief plotted, nothing's estranged.
The funny things that make us smile,
Guarded closely, our heart's own style.

Glorious Hues of Affection

In a realm where colors dance and play,
A heart-shaped gem decided to sway.
Red like ketchup, blue like a sky,
It sparkled and winked, oh my, oh my!

With every hue, a story unfurled,
A green for the cabbage saving the world.
Yellow for laughter, orange for fun,
It giggled and sparkled, oh what a run!

Friends gathered round, all clad in cheer,
They couldn't stop laughing at tales so dear.
The gem told a joke, a polka dot prank,
And suddenly, it turned into a tank!

So if you find yourself feeling blue,
Just wear a gem, it'll brighten your view.
With glorious hues, affection shall rise,
In a rainbow of laughter, under sunny skies!

A Shimmer of the Past

Once there was a charm, quite silly indeed,
With stories of love and chocolate and greed.
It shimmered so bright, with secrets it kissed,
But lost all its shine in a misty twist.

"What happened?" it asked, while floating around,
"I used to make hearts leap, quite profound!"
Friends brought back a cupcake, a blast from the past,
The sparkle returned, and suddenly—fast!

With frosting and sprinkles, the charm gave a cheer,
Bouncing on bubbles, spreading good cheer.
"Let's party!" it shouted, with a wiggle and dance,
Inviting all memories to join in the prance!

So gather your stories, both funny and bright,
For a shimmer of laughter can set hearts alight.
With a wink and a chuckle, take a trip down the lane,
For past joys will come, like a sweet candy rain!

Stars in the Palm

In the palm of your hand, a universe sways,
With stars made of glitter and funny ways.
A twinkling comet slipped on a shoe,
And landed right here—it chuckled, who knew?

"Do you see me shine?" it sparkled with glee,
"Just watch me dance, and you will agree!"
With flips and with flops, it leaped in the night,
Telling tales of adventures, the moonshiny light.

A galaxy gathered, with planets all smiles,
They played hide and seek over cosmic miles.
"Your palm is a stage!" they laughed in delight,
As laughter burst forth like a comet in flight!

So let your hand hold the stars you adore,
Each giggle and twinkle brings joy evermore.
With stories of whimsy, and funny delight,
The universe shines in the palm of your light!

Vows Under Starlight

Under a sky, with stars all aglow,
Two silly hearts made a vow—a show!
"I promise to dance like a chicken tonight,
And wear mismatched socks, oh what a sight!"

In whispers and giggles, the promise was made,
To twirl like a dervish, unafraid.
With vows that included a pie-eating race,
Under the glitter, they laughed in embrace.

"Let's waltz with the moon, or maybe cha-cha,
With dreams painted loud, like a jazzy piñata!"
So they leaped and they spun, bodies a-whirl,
Making vows of hilarity, with every swirl.

Together in laughter, they embraced the night,
A whimsical echo of love so bright.
With vows under starlight, so silly and true,
They promised a life filled with fun, just for two!

The Heart's Hidden Glow.

In a pocket, small and round,
Lives a treasure that I found.
When I hold it, sparks just fly,
Like a firework up in the sky.

Friends all laugh, they pry and tease,
"What's inside? Come on, please!"
I just grin and hide away,
My heart's glow is here to stay.

When it twinkles, joy ignites,
Dancing shadows, silly sights.
I do a jig with silly feet,
Letting silliness take the seat.

Oh that charm, so small and bright,
Keeps the giggles, lights the night.
With each flicker, laughter swells,
In this pocket lies my spells.

Glimmers of Memory.

A little trinket, oh so grand,
With secrets tucked beneath my hand.
It winks at me with glee and cheer,
I swear it knows my deepest fear.

Each gleam's a story, wild and bold,
Of goofy moments, tales retold.
One time I slipped on a banana peel,
This tiny gem could make it real!

With every shimmer, laughter grows,
It knows my quirks, my silly woes.
Like a magician's finest act,
It keeps the joy, that's a fact!

Oh, what fun this little charm brings,
Reminding me of silly things.
It sparkles bright, a tiny sun,
With a wink, it just says, "Run!"

Heartstrings Unfurled.

In my pocket, snuggled tight,
Is a charm that beams so bright.
It tickles my heart with every shine,
As if to say, "Life is divine!"

It whispers tales of days gone past,
Of silly hats and how long they last.
A dance-off with a cat or two,
Who'd have thought this was my crew?

Each flicker's like a tiny spark,
Illuminating all the dark.
With puns and quips, it keeps me near,
And fills my heart with endless cheer.

So here I prance, my heart so free,
With my gem, just wait and see!
Together we'll twirl and spin around,
With laughter as our only sound.

Illuminated Whispers.

A glinting gem within my grasp,
Whispers secrets, makes me gasp.
It twirls and dances, oh what a sight,
Bringing giggles deep into the night.

In crowded rooms, it shines so bold,
Sharing stories that need to be told.
Like a parrot on a funny spree,
This charm knows all my history.

Every flicker, a joke is spun,
I laugh until I'm on the run.
With silly faces and random prance,
This charm says, "Come on, let's dance!"

So if you find this tiny light,
Join me in the giggly night.
With every laugh and every cheer,
We'll make sweet memories year after year!

Radiance in Remembrance

In a dusty drawer, I found a bright ring,
Its shine was the opposite of a bear's fling.
I swore it spoke secrets, whispered out loud,
To all the bad jokes I never allowed.

It glinted and winked, a mischievous tease,
Reminded me of milk spills and careless bees.
Holding my laughs, a treasure untold,
This glowing trinket, a friend made of gold.

Secrets of the Heart

A heart-shaped pendant, oh what could it hold?
A recipe for laughter, or maybe for gold?
I peeked inside, it just had a note,
Saying, "Life's too short, so just grab a coat!"

Its mysteries squeaked like a chipmunk in flight,
Searching for chuckles on a dark starry night.
Patting my pocket, it jiggled with glee,
Saying, "I'll lighten your load, just take me with thee!"

Shimmering Echoes

In the corner, it sparkled, a star in disguise,
Echoes of giggles, like popcorn surprise.
I gave it a shake, and out came some flair,
Dance moves and laughter floated in the air.

The echoes were sticky, like jam on a toast,
A trap for the serious, I'd cheerfully boast.
Every shine's a joke, a friend in the night,
Together we twinkle, what a splendid sight!

A Flash of Gold

A flash of gold caught my coy little eye,
It grinned like a cat, oh my, oh my!
With a wink and a nod, it shared a good pun,
"Why did the chicken? Oh wait, let's run!"

It told me of parties held deep in a sock,
Where toast was a dance, and cheese was a rock.
I laughed till I cried, a bright shining jest,
This bit of my past just made me feel blessed.

The Charm of Faded Photographs

In an old album, a cat wears a hat,
Grinning wide, oh, what of that!
A fish in a bowl, with a monocle too,
Staring at us, like it knew what to do.

Grandpa in suspenders, just dancing away,
He tripped on his feet, oh what a display!
A sock on his hand, he thought it was neat,
We laugh at the memories, oh what a treat!

A dog in a tux, with a bow tie so bold,
Chasing its tail, what stories are told.
The colors may fade, the moments stay bright,
Each snapshot a giggle, a burst of delight.

So let's flip the pages, let laughter take flight,
At the charm of these faces, so silly and light.
For in every behold, there's joy to unshroud,
In the charm of the past, we'll say it out loud!

Light Captured in Clasped Hands

In a pocket of jeans lies a treasure, oh dear,
Tiny toys, from when we had cheer.
A gummy bear, lost, but still with a grin,
As if saying, 'I'm still ready to win!'

A marble that twinkles, like stars in the night,
Held tightly in palms, oh, what a sight!
We giggle and squabble, who gets to decide,
Whose turn for the marble? Oh, what a ride!

A paperclip sculpture, so funky and proud,
It holds all our notes, like a quirky crowd.
The laughter unfolds, as we bond in our quest,
To find simple treasures, oh, we are so blessed.

So clasp your hands tight, feel the joy, feel the cheer,
In the light of connection, there's nothing to fear.
For the treasures we hold, in our hearts and our hands,
Bring laughter and fun, like faraway lands!

The Beauty of What Remains

Dusty old trinkets, a shoe and a shoe lace,
The remnants of laughter, time won't erase.
A half-eaten cookie, a lovably stale,
Each piece tells a tale, in giggles we sail.

A button so big, like a plate on our clothes,
Stitched with high hopes, as the hilarity grows.
Giggles erupt when the odd ones we find,
In the beauty of chaos, we're blissfully blind.

A cereal box with a dinosaur prize,
Fortresses built, under pillows that rise.
With each little laugh, we pull memories tight,
In the beauty of moments, everything's right.

So cherish the little, let love intertwine,
In remnants of laughter, our hearts truly shine.
For the beauty that lingers, in jest and in play,
Makes every endeavor, a wonderfully bright day!

Gems of Yesterday's Heart

A rubber band ball, so splendidly round,
Bouncing about, oh, what joy it found!
Each twist and each turn, a story it tells,
Of laughter and foolishness, inside jokes, and spells.

A sticky note stuck, on a cat's fluffy head,
The notes that we used had become quite widespread.
Our plans written down, all jumbled and fun,
A treasure map drawn to the next silly pun!

A glittery pen that ran dry long ago,
Yet in its lost ink, the memories flow.
Each scratch and each doodle, a giggle infused,
In the gems of our hearts, we rejoice and peruse.

So let's seek out the gems, let laughter be bright,
In the hearts of the past, there's always more light.
For in every lost moment, a jewel can be found,
With the smiles and the fun, our spirits are crowned!

A Pendant's Promise

In a shiny trinket with tales to weave,
Promises of laughter, you best believe.
It jangles and jingles like a cat in flight,
Whispering secrets in the dead of night.

A squirrel once wore it, thought it a crown,
He danced through the park, trying not to drown.
But oh, how it sparkles, despite all the fuss,
Who knew a pendant could cause such a fuss?

The Secrets That Sparkle

Twinkling trinkets, a gossip's delight,
Spilling the beans, oh what a sight!
They chuckle and giggle like friends at a feast,
'If I had arms, I'd wave like the least!'

A rumor's afoot in their glimmering dance,
Who wore it to dinner? Who dared take a chance?
Echoes of laughter wrapped in a chain,
Bringing back memories, both silly and plain.

Nostalgia Wrapped in Delicate Chains

Each link a memory, winks from the past,
A sticky mishap that just couldn't last.
A woeful mishap with an ice cream cone,
Brought giggles and grumbles, like an old-timey phone.

Rummaging through boxes, oh what a sight,
Finding a charm that shimmers so bright.
It winks at the wearer, 'Remember the day?'
When fashion was daring, in a ridiculous way!

Dazzling Echoes of the Past

A bauble of joy, it swings to and fro,
Revealing the secrets of long ago.
With each little jingle, a chuckle escapes,
As memories bounce like a cat on shapes.

A story unfolds from a long-lost bling,
Of mischief and mayhem, just taking wing.
'Twas worn by a goat who fancied a dance,
Leaving us giggling at sartorial chance.

Remnants of Forgotten Ties

In pockets deep, a treasure hides,
Forgotten scraps of tangled rides.
A paperclip, a twisty tie,
Glimpses of joy that once flew by.

The rubber band, all stretched and worn,
Remember when it held the corn?
An old receipt from last week's spree,
Proof that I once shopped for free!

A napkin note with doodles galore,
Of pizza nights we can't ignore.
But what's this thing? A crumbled mint!
My breath says yes, my heart says glint!

So here I sit, with crumbs and quirks,
Among the remnants of lost works.
I'll laugh and sigh, and maybe cry,
For silly ties that still comply.

Embraced by Warmth

A sweater too small, I still wear it with pride,
Worn backwards and frayed, it's my favorite guide.
Its sleeves slip off, I stumble and dance,
Yet every misstep leads to a chance!

The socks that don't match, a game I still play,
One's green like a frog, the other, well, gray.
They keep my toes snug; who cares what they see?
In this comical fashion, I'm wild and I'm free!

Hot cocoa spills on my shirt, oh what fun!
I giggle and grin as I race to the sun.
With marshmallows bouncing, like hugs from above,
I dance in the chaos, all wrapped up in love.

Like clouds in a jumble, I float without care,
In a whirlwind of warmth, I'll go anywhere.
With friends by my side, it's a riotous show,
Embraced by the warmth, together we glow!

Hidden Gems

In a drawer, a treasure trove waits,
Laughing at receipts from long-gone dates.
Old birthday cards with scribbles inside,
Who knew I could doodle and still not provide?

A patch from summer camp's wildest scheme,
I sewed it on strange—what a whimsical dream!
Beads from a bracelet that fell to the floor,
Worn by a monster, I'll smile and explore.

A bottle cap claiming to be a key,
Not for a lock, but a mystery spree.
These hidden gems tell tales in the night,
Of silly adventures—oh, what a delight!

So let's toast to the treasures that clutter our space,
With laughter and fun, it's a charming embrace.
For every odd trinket that makes our hearts swell,
Is a piece of the magic in our living hell!

Illuminated Journeys

Under the streetlamp's golden glow,
I tripped on a cat, and to laughter I flowed.
With friends in a circle, we shared our tall tales,
Like Ace in a race, we sailed like the gales.

A path made of giggles and wobbly rides,
With maps made of napkins, we took joyful strides.
"Where are we going?" we'd laugh and we'd cheer,
As the moon played the DJ, we danced without fear.

With costumes and quirks, like a circus parade,
We twirled through the night till the dawn began frayed.
Each stumble a sparkle, each mishap a jest,
In this illuminated journey, we felt truly blessed.

So let's scribble our stories on pages of glow,
For each winding road leads to laughter we sow.
With hearts like a lighthouse, we'll beacon our way,
In the glow of our memories, forever we'll stay!

Light Beneath the Surface

In pockets deep, a glint does hide,
A secret charm, with glee inside.
It whispers tales of bright delight,
And plays with shadows in the night.

With playful spark, it twirls about,
A little laugh that joins the rout.
It finds the socks that miss their pair,
And winks at those who stop and stare.

A catch of dust, a laughing glow,
It steals the show with cheeky show.
A twinkle here, a giggle there,
A dancing flicker, light as air.

So keep it close, this glowing friend,
For even socks find joy to lend.
With every chuckle, every grin,
It lights the way for fun to win.

Fragments of Solar Dreams

Crumbs of sunshine, brightly spilled,
In oddball shapes, our laughter's thrilled.
Each little spark, a silly tease,
A flash of whimsy in the breeze.

Like pencils drawn on paper skies,
They sketch the silliness that flies.
A moonlit giggle, morning's cheer,
These glowing bits are ever near.

A jellybean of dreams gone wild,
They hop and skip, the rays beguiled.
In every corner, giggles hide,
A messy joy, both bright and wide.

Collecting all these frisky beams,
Together blend our crazy dreams.
With every shimmer, every jest,
Sweet laughter lives, we are so blessed.

Emblazoned Connections

In tangled strings of gooey cheer,
Connections dance, a bright veneer.
With every knot, a smile is tied,
As glowworms laugh and warm inside.

This jumbled mess of winks and grins,
A choo-choo train where laughter wins.
They skip and hop, a flaming train,
With every squeal, a joyous gain.

With silly songs and twinkly beams,
They paint our world with vivid dreams.
Bright sunshine hugs the tangled threads,
And silly thoughts dance in our heads.

So here we stand, a funny crew,
With radiant sparks in every hue.
Emblazoned hearts, forever bold,
In laughter's warmth, our tale is told.

Beacon of Lost Conversations

In shadows deep, where whispers play,
A beacon's laugh will light the way.
With echoes bright of words once said,
It tickles thoughts that dance in dread.

A comet's wink, a wisecrack here,
Light bounces off, it pulls us near.
The chatter breaks, a giggle spills,
As stories weave with jolly thrills.

We chase the beams, we twirl around,
In lost conversations, joy is found.
Each chuckle swells, each jest ignites,
A beacon glows on starry nights.

So round we go, this merry band,
In laughter's arms, we make our stand.
For every light, a tale to share,
A beacon's warmth is everywhere.

Whispered Treasures

In my pocket, a secret, oh so bright,
It giggles and chuckles, a pure delight.
A tiny glow dances, like a firefly,
Telling silly tales, making me sigh.

This treasure of laughter, I hold so near,
It whispers sweet jokes that bring me cheer.
With every quick glance, it shines from below,
Winks at the world, just stealing the show.

Where did it come from? I have no clue,
Maybe a goblin, or perhaps a shoe?
But when I'm feeling low, it's my little muse,
A spark of joy that I cannot refuse.

So here's to the wonders that keep us amused,
A pocket of giggles, forever infused.
A trinket of smiles, so snug in my mix,
My tiny delight, it's a funny fix!

Glowing Testaments

A charm that radiates with goofy glee,
In shadows it whispers, oh can't you see?
It tells clumsy stories of trips and spills,
Of matching the dough with the bravest of thrills.

Its shimmer's contagious, it tickles my heart,
Each glow is a laugh, a delightful art.
With friends at my side and this gem in hand,
We bask in the glow of the silly planned.

Through laughter we find a bright little tale,
That silliness always will surely prevail.
Oh, how it twinkles with a wink and a grin,
Turning mundane moments to whimsical spins.

As the day turns to night, still laughs we ignite,
Chasing shadows and giggles with pure delight.
This glowing token, a testament true,
With belly laughs heard, and joy ever new!

A Pocket of Light

In a pocket of nonsense, I find my joy,
A bubbly surprise, a giggling toy.
It springs in my hand, doing cartwheels and flips,
Making my day with its wiggly quips.

A shimmer of laughter, a dash of the bold,
It shares all the secrets that never get old.
With friends by my side, we unleash the fun,
A madcap adventure has only begun.

It glows like a beacon, a playful light,
Guiding us forth into the wild night.
With every small giggle and over-the-top cheer,
A pocket of joy, it banishes fear.

So let's raise a toast to these moments so bright,
To the pockets of magic that give us delight.
With bursts of pure laughter and silliness spun,
A tale full of sparkles where we all run!

Chasing the Radiant

We chase the absurd like kids on a spree,
With chase after laughter, it's all just so free.
This radiant beacon, no need for a guide,
It dances on air with a silly pride.

Through puddles and giggles, we leap with glee,
Chasing the glow that keeps calling to me.
A sprinkle of whimsy, a dash of the weird,
With each step of joy, we're terribly cheered.

Under stars that twinkle, we laugh and we roam,
In search of the funny, we always feel home.
From whispers to roars, our delight is a song,
With our silly treasure, where we all belong.

So here's to the chase, the joy we ignite,
With every laugh shared, the world feels so bright.
For moments that matter, we let passion swing,
Chasing the smile that our memories bring!

Iridescent Ties That Bind

In a chest of treasures, I found a charm,
It winked at my heart, and caused quite the alarm.
A nephew in hand-me-downs, wearing my dreams,
I realized that old jokes are never as it seems.

A cat with a collar, oh what a disgrace,
Stealing my locket to wear on his face.
He pranced around proudly, a feline with flair,
And I just stood laughing, too shocked to declare.

Then I saw the dog, full of mischief and fun,
Chasing the cat, oh what moments undone!
Who needs a treasure, with friends like these,
Turning days into jest, with giggles to please.

So here's to the baubles that bring us delight,
May they glimmer and shimmer, like stars in the night.
For in every mishap, and every small fight,
Laughter's the gem, and we're all feeling bright.

A Keepsake's Silent Song

I once had a trinket, a piece of old gold,
It jingled with secrets and stories untold.
A dance in the kitchen, it slipped from my grip,
And my cat dove right in, with a mischievous flip.

I chased it around like a clown on a spree,
While my neighbors peered out, chuckling at me.
With a leap and a bound, it rolled near the floor,
That shiny old treasure was lost in the roar.

Oh, the laughter I gathered from all of this mess,
A keepsake of giggles, oh what a success!
So if you have a charm that's causing you strife,
Just laugh till you cry—it's the best kind of life!

In echoes of memories, may humor resound,
For every lost treasure, true mirth can be found.
So wear laughter boldly, through ups and through downs,
And cherish the moments that bring forth the clowns.

Hope Embodied in Precious Metal

A ring on my finger, it sparkles and glows,
I thought it had wisdom, but where did it go?
In pockets and purses, it used to reside,
Now it's lost in the couch, along with my pride.

I called my dog over, with eyes full of hope,
"Did you eat my shiny? Oh, please don't mope!"
He woofed with a grin, said, "It's all in good fun,
But you'll find it in spring, after winter is done."

So, I laughed at his words, and we tumbled around,
Playing hide and seek with the lost keepsake found.
Each little mishap is a lesson, I know,
That joy in the journey brings light as we go.

As ages pass by and treasures all fade,
It's the giggles and moments that never degrade.
So hold tight your laughter, let merriment swell,
For hope's in our hearts, more than any old bell.

Luminescence of Love Lost

A necklace once worn, it had stories to tell,
Now it's hiding somewhere, oh where could it dwell?
I searched every drawer and beneath every bed,
My heart made a plan, but my head just said red.

Then came a surprise, a gift from my mate,
A sock with a charm, oh what a twisted fate!
I laughed at the thought, as I wore it with pride,
Who knew that my treasure would come in disguise?

The cat did a dance, it was quite a grand sight,
With my sock on its head, it brought me delight.
We twirled and we giggled, through day into night,
For love's not a trinket, but shines oh so bright.

In moments of laughter, the heart beats alive,
For every lost pendant, new joys will arrive.
So cherish the whimsy, let silliness flow,
And in the dark corners, let humor bestow.

The Timeless Spark

In a box with a charm so small,
A secret giggle, a mystery call.
It shines bright when I tell a joke,
Turns my cat into a dancing bloke.

Each time I wear, the laughter grows,
On my friend's face, a grin bestows.
But when I pause, it dims just so,
Even my grandma has to glow!

It sparkles bright at silly tales,
Winks at whimsy, no room for fails.
With every chuckle, it beams so wide,
Like a firefly on a joyful ride.

Blingy treasure with a quirky twist,
In every memory, it can't be missed.
From my pocket, it blinks with delight,
A radiant gem, oh what a sight!

Glimpses of Radiance

A sparkly thing in a grand old case,
It whispers jokes, leaves a funny trace.
When I wear it, the world seems right,
Even my shoe starts a dance tonight!

It plays peek-a-boo with the moon,
Tickling stars with a silly tune.
Each time I wear it, laughter flows,
Makes even my dog strike a pose!

With glimmers bright it steals the show,
Turning my coffee into a flow.
Giggling, glowing, it sparks a cheer,
When it's around, there's no room for fear!

In parties and picnics, it never fails,
Hitching rides on my wildest tales.
A glimmering companion, it shines so clear,
Bringing joy to all who come near!

A Memory's Fireside

At the hearth where laughter thrives,
Sits a trinket that always jives.
With every tickle of the flame,
It whispers secrets, plays a game.

Among the friends, it shines so bright,
Lighting up hearts on a chilly night.
A flicker here, a nod from there,
Turns even socks into a bear!

We gather round, all snug and tight,
Each story told puts the spark alight.
A memory dressed in giggles and glee,
It winks and nods, "Hey, look at me!"

A playful shadow on the wall,
In this cozy space, we have a ball.
Fireside shenanigans, all in good fun,
With every chuckle, our hearts run!

Flickers of Forgotten Whispers

In an attic filled with dusty dreams,
A tiny spark giggles and beams.
It recounts tales of cheese and bread,
Of mice that danced, of things unsaid.

Every flicker brings a chuckle forth,
From a land of whimsy, quite north.
With every blink, it stirs the past,
Reminds us how long laughter can last.

It whispers tales from yesteryears,
Of silly hats and endless cheers.
As memories float on its flickering glow,
I can't help but giggle, and let joy flow!

So here's to sparks from days of yore,
To the laughter, silly, and evermore.
In each tiny glow, a fun little twist,
A reminder that joy should always exist!

Luminous Continuity

In the pocket, a curious charm,
Whispers secrets, causing no harm.
Shiny and bright, it attracts the flies,
Buzzing around, oh how time flies!

With each giggle, the charm starts to glow,
Who knew a trinket could put on a show?
It sways like a dancer in midair,
Tickling our hearts with colorful flair.

Friends gather 'round, like moths to the flame,
Each trying to steal the charm's bright name.
A tug-of-war ensues, laughter spills,
As we chase the glow that gives us thrills!

In the end, we just can't keep it in sight,
Melting in giggles, oh what a night!
A glowing moment, forever we'll share,
A memory bright, without a care.

The Guardian's Gleam

A silly guardian stands by my side,
With a grin so big, and eyes open wide.
He wobbles and jigs, oh what a sight,
Guarding my treasures with all of his might!

He waves his hands, making shadows dance,
As I ponder if I'd ever take a chance.
To ask for a wish, but then I would see,
He's just a funny guardian, loving me!

With every burst of laughter we share,
He shines in the dark, dispelling all care.
A glow in his smile, a spark in his stride,
Together, we conquer, a joyful ride!

His giggles echo, like bells in the night,
Reminding me, wrongs can turn to right.
Hold tight to the laughter, it's precious and rare,
With a guardian gleaming, I'll always dare.

The Warmth We Carry

In pockets deep, we gather the smiles,
A warmth that stretches for countless miles.
Each chuckle we share, fuels the flame,
It's our little secret, who's to blame?

A dance with the silliness, we take our stance,
Every twirl and whirl, adds to the chance.
To heat up the chilly corners of life,
With hugs made of humor, and no sign of strife!

We laugh through the storms, we skip through the rain,
Harnessing joy, in our playful domain.
With every bright sparkle we cast to the sky,
We light up the world, you and I!

So cherish the laughter, hold it close at hand,
For it lights up the path, making life grand.
In the warmth of our hearts, we'll always carry,
A joy everlasting, never to tarry.

Threads of Essence

With threads of laughter, we weave a tale,
Stitching together, through giggles we sail.
Each moment a fiber, shimmering bright,
Creating a tapestry, pure delight!

The weaver grins, turning mischief to gold,
Crafting our stories, never too bold.
With every stitch, a memory made,
In the fabric of joy, doubts start to fade.

So come take a seat, it's a party tonight,
Where every mistake turns humor to light!
The essence we share, a blend of our glee,
Threads intertwined, just you and me!

In the laughter's embrace, we'll dance and we'll spin,
Creating a cosmos where joy can begin.
With threads that are woven, our spirits will thrive,
In this funny tapestry, we come alive!

Reflections in a Forgotten Frame

In a drawer with socks and shoes,
Lies a treasure we forgot to choose.
Faded photos and silly grins,
Captured moments where laughter spins.

A cat wearing a tiny hat,
Oh, how he thought he was all that!
Grandpa dancing with a broom,
Dust bunnies soaring 'round the room.

A birthday cake, three tiers tall,
The candles lit; we missed the call.
A faceplant caught in mid-fall glee,
Every mishap a memory!

So here we laugh and sigh with smiles,
As time plays tricks with quirky styles.
In this frame of forgotten fun,
Let's relive what can't be undone!

A Melody of What Once Was

In a world where music stutters,
Grandma sways and mutters 'utters'.
Her old records skip and play,
A charming tune from yesterday.

She croons to socks hung on the line,
Pretending they're a dance divine.
The dog howls, joins in the show,
A cacophony of tail and toe.

In the kitchen, spoons are drums,
The fridge hums back with stubborn thumps.
A polka party, feast and cheer,
Even the vegetables want near!

As laughter rolls through halls of cheer,
A melody we hold so dear.
With each note the past replays,
In giggles and song-filled days!

The Warmth of Remembered Touch

An old quilt stitched with love and tears,
A patchwork of forgotten years.
Each square a tale woven tight,
Of kids and dogs and late-night fright.

A smear of jam on Grandma's face,
She laughed, not worried, not a disgrace.
Furry hats and goofy shoes,
We danced through life with silly views.

The air a buzz with stories spun,
Imaginings of days of fun.
Desserts made only by our hands,
Chocolate rivers and candy lands.

With every hug and gentle squeeze,
The warmth within puts hearts at ease.
In memories, we find our clutch,
These whimsical tales of tender touch!

Enchantment in an Heirloom

A necklace tucked in velvet dreams,
With charms that jingle, giggle, and gleam.
Each trinket tells a tale absurd,
Of magic acts and prankish words.

A spoon that once could stir a pot,
Now makes us giggle on the spot.
Silly stories of pirate lore,
As forks become swords in a playful war.

The old clock chimes with silly tones,
As family gathers, laughter groans.
A treasure found in laughing eyes,
Embracing quirks beneath the skies.

So here we sit, the past in play,
Each heirloom brightens up the gray.
In every chuckle, every sigh,
Magic reigns where memories lie!

Liquid Gold

Once I found a golden flask,
Filled with juice, not whiskey, I ask.
A sip brought giggles, oh what a tease,
Turned my thoughts into buzzing bees.

I danced with cats, under the sun,
Calling them in for some fun.
They pranced and jumped, all good and bold,
Claiming my treasure, my liquid gold.

But as I spun, my drink took flight,
Flying high into the night.
Now the stars twinkle, just my luck,
Sipping starlight, oh what a chuck!

In my golden dreams, I now reside,
With singing squirrels as they glide.
Toasting to joy, I raise my cup,
For this silly life, I can't get enough.

Spiritual Beacons

Two socks prayerfully unmatched,
Alight in heaven, they've attached.
Guiding my feet through the darkest night,
With every waddle, bringing delight.

Balloons float by like thoughts of cheer,
Whispering secrets for all to hear.
They giggle and bounce, sharing good vibes,
Making my soul dance in joyful jibes.

A rubber duck, with a wise old quack,
Navigates life on a wobbly track.
He floats on doesn't care where he goes,
Riding the waves of life's silly shows.

In this funny realm of carefree ways,
I find beacons that spark bright days.
With a chuckle and skip, on this wacky street,
Every haphazard moment feels oh-so sweet.

A Story Enfolded

In a book with pages not yet turned,
A tale of a sock that always yearned.
To find its mate and go on adventures,
Together they'd laugh, with silly ventures.

In the first chapter, they danced on clouds,
Making friends with the fluffiest crowds.
They twirled with laughter, leveled and bold,
Creating a story that never gets old.

The plots got tangled, a maze of fun,
With penguins and ice cream races to run.
Every twist led to giggles and cheer,
As sock and his partner spread joy far and near.

So flip the page, let the laughter unfold,
For in this book, all hearts turn to gold.
Every silly tale, a treasure untold,
In life's grand saga, we laugh, we behold.

Touched by Twilight

As dusk tiptoed with a wink,
My cat donned glasses, made me rethink.
He claimed to see shadows of spaghetti,
Whispering secrets, feeling quite zesty.

The moon wore a hat with stars all around,
Spinning yarns of mischief, they bounced on the ground.
They tickled the trees, made the night sing,
Even the crickets joined in the fling.

A raccoon dressed up in a tuxedo sleek,
Asking me questions, oh so unique.
"Do you believe in fairies?" he said with a grin,
As I pondered, the giggling began to spin.

The twilight giggles wrapped us in delight,
Holding onto moments that danced like light.
So here we are, in this playful dance,
Surrounded by magic, love, and a chance.

Heartstrings Woven in Gold

In a cupboard sat an old tin box,
Hiding secrets and matching socks.
A knickknack here, a trinket there,
Sparkling stories beyond compare.

A shiny charm with a quirky face,
Always seems to win the race.
It giggles loud, it dances light,
In dreams of treasure, oh, what a sight!

Gold threads weave through silly lore,
Like cats that dance on a candy store.
Each memory sings in a lively tune,
Under the gaze of a laughing moon.

So here's to treasures beyond our dreams,
And playtime joys that burst at the seams.
With a wink and a nod, we chase the night,
Chasing shadows in playful delight.

The Glow of Cherished Remembrance

A memory stirs in a tea-stained cup,
Where mismatched spoons are all stacked up.
Each sip reminds of tales once told,
Of wiggles and giggles, shiny and bold.

A dancing cat under a table's leg,
Lickety-split it flips a beg.
With a waggle and wiggle, it joins the fun,
As laughter bursts like the morning sun.

Button-eyed creatures with chubby cheeks,
Share funny heartbeats, like lullaby squeaks.
In every chuckle, there's love that's dear,
Like ticklish whispers for all to hear.

So toast to moments, both silly and sweet,
In the attic of minds where silly things meet.
Each goodbye echoing, as memories flit,
In the playful glow of a starlit skit.

Illuminated Bygone Days

In the attic, there's an old shoe box,
Packed with magic and funny thoughts.
Dust bunnies dance, while memories roar,
With rubber chickens and pranks galore.

A photo of uncles doing the twist,
Caught mid-laugh, how could you miss?
Adding sparkles to the Family Gala,
Oh, we were quite the goofy ballerinas, ta-da!

Each night we'd giggle under the stars,
Dreaming of ice cream and candy bars.
With marshmallow moons and licorice skies,
Our hearts grew light as our laughter flies.

So here's a toast to days gone by,
Filled with silliness that makes us sigh.
Like fireflies twinkling on a warm summer night,
We cherish these moments, forever in flight.

Fragments of a Timeless Bond

A puzzle piece that's always lost,
Hiding beneath the couch like a ghost.
It chuckles soft as it settles snug,
With memories woven, oh what a tug!

Dance like jelly, hop like a frog,
Each silly move is a heartful log.
We scrapbook joy with glitter and glue,
In a whirling world, just me and you.

Whimsical whispers through secret doors,
In a wacky land of laughter roars.
With each silly dance and jiggly jive,
Treasured fragments make our hearts thrive.

So let's skip through sunshine, hand in hand,
With giggly echoes across the land.
For in every chuckle, in every smile,
Lies a timeless bond, so pure and worthwhile.

Treasures Bound in Gilded Threads

In a box beneath the bed,
Are trinkets that I dread.
A rubber band, a ball of lint,
Laughter finds what's hard to hint.

A necklace made of paper clips,
Which wobbles on my silly trips.
With treasures wrapped in such a mess,
Who knew my junk could still impress?

A button bright from grandma's coat,
It sings when I wear my old boat.
This fashion might just start a trend,
Who knew the chuckles it could send?

So here's to treasures, weird and grand,
In every pocket, every hand.
With giggles shared, we find the best,
In gold and junk, we're truly blessed!

A Glint Beneath the Surface

Beneath the couch, a shiny thing,
I reach for joy that dreams can bring.
A spoon, a key, a lost old toy,
Each sparkles with its hidden joy.

I take a sip of fizzy drink,
The bubbles rise, oh, how they wink!
A treasure hunt in my own home,
Who knew such fun I could have grown?

A dented can of soda pop,
It dances as I give a hop.
With every sip, I feel the cheer,
Our funny finds draw loved ones near!

So here's to glints that make us smile,
In every nook, let's search a while.
For laughter glows where none could see,
And treasures hide in mystery!

Secrets Held in Shimmering Embrace

In my pocket rests a prize,
Confetti kissed by sparkling eyes.
A secret stash of silly things,
Like rubber ducks and paper rings.

A note so small with doodles bright,
It teases kin with pure delight.
A jingle bell that shakes with glee,
Resounding tales of mystery.

Each hidden gem, a laugh we find,
With bubbly charm, they intertwine.
They're whispers soft of joy and jest,
In laughter's arms, we feel the best.

So let's embrace the freaky sights,
With secrets sown in silly lights.
With every chuckle, life's a dance,
In shiny hugs, let's take a chance!

Shadows of Distant Love

In shadows cast by flickering lights,
We share our notes like paper kites.
A sock adorned with polka dots,
Spills secrets hidden in its knots.

With every glance, a wink conveyed,
In playful jests, our fears allayed.
Through shadows thick, our laughter flows,
Like silly gnomes with twitchy toes.

When love's a game of peek-a-boo,
We chase the laughs till skies are blue.
With every whisper, joy can gleam,
In shadows bold, we dare to dream.

So here's to love that makes us grin,
In quirky tales, we always win.
With every giggle, let's embark,
For shadows hold our brightest spark!

Love's Timeless Flicker

In a drawer, a relic sleeps,
With memories in whispers deep.
A couple's grin, a pinch of flair,
It holds their joy beyond compare.

But open it—what's this? A sock?
Did love take a detour, round the block?
The heart still dances, oh so spry,
With mismatched thoughts that make us sigh.

Time bends with laughter, oh how it sways,
When trinkets tell of silly days.
Yet love persists, a silly game,
That flickers on, forever the same.

So clumsy love's memories, hold them tight,
In a cherished frame, they shine so bright!
A laugh, a glance, a moment silly,
Flickering joy, never too frilly.

A Tinge of Serenity

In the midst of chaos, a treasure shines,
Wrapped in giggles and silly lines.
A cup of tea, a slice of pie,
Thoughts like bubbles in the sky.

With friends nearby, we revel in cheer,
Bantering tales they long to hear.
A peace that settles, laughter unfolds,
In every moment, more joy it holds.

RESTing heart, no burdened weight,
A waltz of wit, a twist of fate.
We chase the mundane, make it divine,
Serenity found in a playful line.

So here's a toast, to joy that flows,
In silly antics, our gratitude grows!
For in this laughter, our spirits play,
Creating calm in a humorous way.

Resplendence in Shadow

Beneath the couch, where light won't creep,
A glimmer hides, where dust bunnies leap.
A love note lost, with doodles so grand,
    It talks of dreams drawn in the sand.

In shadows lurk, the tales of time,
Of shoe mishaps and fruity chime.
Each wrinkled paper, a memory spry,
    Whispers of laughter, drifting by.

Glimmers twinkle, in corners just right,
Where mischief brews and sparks ignite.
In gentle darkness, we find delight,
Finding resplendence in silly blight.

Oh, how the shadows dance and play,
With all their quirks that save the day!
A treasure trove of the most absurd,
Is where our hearts' laughter is stirred.

The Radiant Archive

In a cupboard, a trove of sights,
Worn-out shoes and funny tights.
Each piece a tale, a giggle rare,
History wrapped in a big bear's stare.

Old photos lay with brows in frowns,
Clownish faces and floppy crowns.
Still, memories whisper, 'Do not fear!
Laughter's the rhythm to bring you cheer!'

A time machine where silliness reigns,
As we recall all the silly gains.
So let's embrace, the quirk in the past,
With each story, our humor steadfast.

In this archive, we dive so deep,
Finding treasures that make us leap!
For a laugh's like sunlight on a park,
Illuminating joy, a cheerful spark.

Glinting Tales of Yesteryears

A shiny disk from days gone by,
I swiped it fast, oh me, oh my.
It caught the sun like a cheeky wink,
I wore it out to make folks think.

Grandma said it held her dreams,
But really it held all her creams.
I wore it proud at the county fair,
Till a goat on the loose gave it a scare!

It twinkled bright as I ran away,
That silly goat just wanted to play.
But as I laughed and lost my breath,
I wondered if that disk meant my death!

Now in the drawer it sits and shines,
With memories sweet like light-hearted wines.
Oh, tales of glinting with laughter shared,
What bizarre adventures I once dared!

A Symphony of Glows

A pendant hums a silly tune,
That dances gently 'neath the moon.
I wear it sparking in the night,
It seems to giggle in delight!

Each sparkle seems to tell a joke,
Like how I tripped on dreams I spoke.
It glimmers with a wink so sly,
Reminding me when I tried to fly!

With every flash, my past appears,
Like the time I serenaded deers.
They didn't clap, just ran away,
Oh, the dreams I had that day!

So here I strut with gleeful pride,
This glowing charm is my goofy guide.
In a world of blunders and fun unknown,
It fizzes joy in every tone!

Threads of Light

There's magic woven in this thread,
I tell you tales of what it said.
It glows at night with vibrant cheer,
Like telling secrets only I hear!

One time it led me on a quest,
To find a snack, oh, what a test!
It blinked and sparkled, showed the way,
To find the cake that made my day!

Now every slice we share with friends,
Are moments where the laughter bends.
I raise a fork to my shining guide,
With crumbs of joy I cannot hide!

So here's to threads that glow so bright,
That weave together our silly night.
With every twinkle, laugh, and bite,
They bring us joy, our hearts take flight!

Emotive Embers

In a pocket lies a glowing spark,
That makes me giggle in the dark.
It's not a gem, nor precious stone,
Just a light that won't leave me alone.

One time I tried to show it off,
To impress a friend, what a goofball scoff!
The light blinked twice and then it died,
My heart was light, but my pride was fried!

Yet here it is, still by my side,
An ember's charm, my fun-filled guide.
With every glimmer, I start to grin,
It's a trusty friend through thick and thin!

So I chuckle at the night's delight,
With an ember glowing, all feels right.
For every joke and twinkling laugh,
My heart ignites, oh what a path!

www.ingramcontent.com/pod-product-compliance
Lightning Source LLC
Chambersburg PA
CBHW070310120526
44590CB00017B/2615